Reaching
the Sun

Books by April Green:

Bloom for Yourself
Bloom for Yourself II, Let go and grow
Becoming a Wildflower
Bloom for Yourself Journal

www.bloomforyourself.co.uk

Reaching
the Sun

April Green

'There's one of April's poems before every chapter of my book Gracefully You

[…] I'm obsessed with her work'

Jenna Dewan

Cover Artwork:
Bea & Wild

Illustrations:
Bea & Wild
Instagram: @bea.andwild

ISBN: 978-1-5272-8561-3

www.bloomforyourself.co.uk

It's okay if you're not yet
where you want to be.

Remember:

You don't always notice
the sun rising in the sky
until, one day, you feel
its warmth touching your face
and you realise how much
you have grown.

love, april green

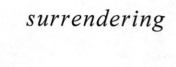

surrendering

A note from the author

When I started the journey of becoming the woman I knew I deserved to be, the woman I was designed to be, she felt familiar. I realised that I wasn't discovering a new person, but rather uncovering my essential self: the person I was before the world taught me who to be.

The concept I had of myself growing up, and well into adulthood, was constructed from low self-worth and limited beliefs; as though I had placed a barrier around myself that (I believed) I couldn't remove.

We all have deep rooted beliefs and narratives; all of them come from childhood, conditioning, and experiences. We rarely challenge them because we believe they give us our identity, and if we ever dared to unlearn them, we would lose this identity.

But, for some people like me, we have to lose this identity in order to survive, because it's a false identity; it's not who we truly are. It's who we were told to be, who we were expected to be, who we thought we needed to be in order to live a happy life. And it's only when we start suffocating in shame, feel we're to blame, pull apart the skin we're in, that we notice we're on the wrong path. Everyone looks the same, everyone thinks and speaks the same, everyone loves and hates the same things. We have inadvertently blended in instead of quietly standing out. The passions we had, the individuality we were carving out, the lives we'd started creating, abandoned at the edge of a path that was always meant for us.

April Green

You deserve to live the life that breaks you wide open and scatters your soul into all the places it longs to go. You deserve to live the life where you get to be who you want to be, love what you want to love, and think what you want to think. All because you know where you're going, you know what you need, and you're not afraid to create your own beautiful world. And even if your journey is not the easiest of journeys; even if it feels as though you're travelling through a storm above a calm breeze, you know who you are. You know who you are.

I hope this book helps as a reminder along the way.

Love, April Green

April Green

Living with low self-worth

When you carry around limiting beliefs about yourself, your life plays out in front of a backdrop that taints everything you think, and say, and feel. You rarely get to experience yourself in a full and radiant light. Instead, you learn how to live in the wings, always a few steps behind yourself, never in the centre of your life. You learn behaviours to make you feel something. You learn behaviours to make you feel nothing at all. You swallow your emotions, press your heart to the back of your spine, and tear off pieces of soul. You become silent. You wilt.

(It took me years to believe I deserved to bloom like everyone else.)

April Green

Settling for a life of pain and limiting beliefs
blocks the path for the right things to reach you.

Settling for a life of pain and limiting beliefs
is not what the Universe planned for you.

April Green

Understanding the damage of limiting beliefs

When you accept the false beliefs you have created about yourself, you inadvertently agree to them as the truth, and this determines how you experience everything life has to offer you. But a deeper part of you knows these beliefs are not true, and so a life of inner destruction and torment begins:

Each time you say negative and critical things about yourself, you feel guilty and ashamed.

Each time you focus on the defeats, you reject your achievements.

Each time you think other people are better than you, you shrink to validate that belief.

You start to develop a sense of deep inadequacy in everything you do.

You don't feel good enough for anything you do.

You feel sad, depressed, anxious, and angry.

You blame yourself.

April Green

Please find the courage to reject
your negative belief system
and start again.

April Green

Finding balance

Sometimes, the identity you have built
around yourself
is the very thing that's holding you back.

It's okay to empty yourself of everything
you thought you knew and start again.

And even though you may stumble,
and shudder,
and swallow the wrong things whole;
you will get to taste the sweeter life.

You will get to understand that when
you're surrounded by darkness
you can still have the honey and the light.

April Green

Without positive, healthy self-esteem,
you will never get to experience how valuable you are
to yourself, and the world in which you belong.

April Green

Understanding the energy of low self-worth

Energy connects to like-energy: people are drawn to each other's frequencies.

If you believe you're not good enough, then you will attract people into your space who treat you as though you're not good enough.

That's what the energy of low-self-worth does: it allows others to step into your own private battlefield and keep your false beliefs very much alive.

Seeing yourself through the eyes
of limiting beliefs
leaves you as a fragile, frightened being
in a world that feels too tough,
and too destructive.

But the world is a soft, fluid breath of gold,
and you are the water that falls from her mouth.

You must try and swim to the surface
and look at yourself through her eyes.

(Perspective.)

April Green

Breaking something open

It's terrifying to think that other people's views and opinions can reach into your bones and move you towards a life you're not designed to live. But somehow, that's what my life started to look like: the world I (unconsciously) created for myself was built from ideals that did not come from my soul. I began travelling so far from myself in the process of finding ways to like myself, accept myself, find happiness, that I eventually self-destructed.

And that's sometimes how change starts: you fall, you break, you open yourself so fully that you have no other option than to set free everything you believe to be true and start again.

April Green

Understand that the negative things
people say to you can sometimes stay with you
and create a belief that was never yours
to begin with.

April Green

Becoming unmoved

Unkind words do not hold any power of their own. But if you believe the words that are said to you: if you put feeling and meaning into them; if you allow them to absorb into your skin like the salt of falling tears, then they can cause you everlasting harm. Don't allow unkind words to become your experience—transcend them and see just how valuable you are as the person beneath the veil of every old and limiting belief. For I promise there will come a day when you are so grounded and stable in your relationship with yourself, that you will understand that other people's words mostly convey the relationship they have with themselves.

April Green

Some pain is too heavy to carry;
too traumatic to lift to the surface.

You are allowed to leave some pain where it is
and find a different way to navigate the journey
back to yourself.

April Green

Revealing the wounds

You can't wash away overnight all the years of harming yourself with your thoughts about yourself. You can't fold back the earth and remove the heavy steps you took to walk through each season. There are places inside that are still wounded, and sometimes you won't even remember what you've buried until the same wound reminds you: 'This situation is harming me, these words are hurting me, I need air, I need an exit.'

It's okay to take your time healing from the deeper wounds. It's okay to defend yourself against painful feelings that arise from these wounds. But it's also a good time to acknowledge that you have suffered pain and trauma in your life; that you have deep wounds that need to be healed, that only you can heal them.

April Green

The fear of not being good enough,
of not fitting in, of not being liked,
pulls you away from the value
you are trying so hard to place
upon yourself.

April Green

Pleasing others at the expense of yourself

I learned to live my life trying to meet other people's expectations of me: of what I thought they wanted from me before they would accept me.

When you want to be accepted by everyone, you become a people pleaser; but worst of all, you aim for perfection in every aspect of yourself. You become so attached to the illusion of perfection that you leave behind the very core of who you are: your soul, your values, your wholeness; in search of all the pieces you imagine to be missing.

You roam the Earth looking for answers when the symphony of truth has been playing inside your heart all along.

April Green

And even if you could reach the shiniest, most perfect looking star in the galaxy: you would miss the thousand other stars you passed along the way.

(Release your attachment to the idea of perfection and you will open the door to the whole of the Universe.)

April Green

Lack of self-worth
is a body shrinking
and hiding to be rid of itself.

Lack of self-worth
is an aching to make perfect
everything you think is not.

April Green

Until you get past the mental concept
of who you think you need to be
in order to live a fulfilling life,
you will just keep shrinking and hiding
from who you really are.

April Green

Perfection

Perfection is an idea you have in your mind of something you think will hold the key to happiness. And when you can't seem to reach the unreachable state of perfection, you start blaming yourself, rejecting yourself, and punishing the physical parts of yourself you believe to be holding you back. You start to change, you start to run, you forget who you are, you get so lost in a storm of self-destruction that you can no longer see reality. You shrink and hide in all the dark places because you think your body, your face, your personality are letting you down. You turn to behaviours and habits that keep you from remembering that you don't fit into the person you're so desperate to be.

But you forget that you are only ever supposed to fit into the person you already are.

Aiming for perfection is self-rejection.

The next time you look for perfection outside of yourself,
remember that you're telling the Universe that you believe
you're not worth investing in; that you would rather abandon
yourself in search of something better.

April Green

Dismantling the idea of perfection

You must learn to forgive yourself
for ever believing that perfection
is as real as your beating heart;
that perfection can be reached,
touched, held, worn on top of your skin.

When you remove your perceptions,
and illusions about what you judge as perfect,
you are left with this:

You are here:

you are worthy and unique,
you are on this planet for a reason,
you are sharing your essence with the world,
you are capable of creating incredible,
beautiful things.

April Green

The feelings we hide
cause the most sensitive
wounds.

April Green

Allow the Earth to heal you

I know it feels safe in your inner world:
you can pretend everything is fine,
even when you're falling apart.

But hiding your feelings gets heavy;
and there comes a time when
you have to surrender them to the Earth
and watch them drift away
like the echo of falling rain.

April Green

Some sadness stops time:
it steals your breath away,
grips it tight in its hands
until you're forced to feel it;
until you fall to your knees
and find the strength to
transform.

April Green

Suppressing feelings

I spent years suppressing my feelings; denying them, pushing them deeper and deeper into the silence and stillness of my body because I was terrified of what they meant, and what I should do with them if they ever resurfaced.

But buried feelings cannot settle into new life.

Expressing your true feelings (of shame, and guilt, and fear), through speaking, dancing, writing, and creating, helps you understand what triggers these feelings. It helps you find the reasons why you feel unable to confront them. It helps you work through them.

When you start uncovering your true feelings, you start the process of owning them, understanding them, and taking responsibility for them. You start dismantling the wall that's been separating you from your real, authentic self.

You start living without limitations.

April Green

That thing inside you
that you are running from;
the thing you are trying to escape.
Find out what it is: confront it.
Find out what it wants you to learn.

(Nothing can be loved fully
until you fully own your pain.)

April Green

Owning the wild and hidden parts

I used to be drawn to the darkness in others—the pull of something familiar—part connection, part mystery. I would fall into it, drown in it, become consumed by it in the hope that it would make me feel more whole. But when I found the light within me, I realised that the darkness I was drawn to was simply my own darkness reflected in another.

It can take many painful years to learn that the shadows you see in others reflect the darkness in yourself. But there will come a time when you find the strength to meet yourself so deeply that you will understand these wild and hidden parts. And you will come to love them for what they will teach you:

that the only person you need to fall into is yourself.

April Green

The day I discovered that the beliefs
I had about myself could be changed,
was the day I entered the gate
to my own garden.

April Green

Becoming who you are

When you have the courage
to question your beliefs, you instantly
overpower them with awareness.

You finally come to see that who you truly are
is a free and fearless being who can create
their own narrative, live their own story, and
build their own dreams.

(You become the person you've always wanted to be.)

April Green

Let your past teach you
what it was meant to teach you.

Let it break open a new future
inside you.

April Green

Blooming from the inside

You can start again; you can start from where you are. But you have to do it from the inside out this time. You have to expand beyond the beliefs you have carved into your body, rise above the barrier you have placed upon yourself, create more positive, (and truthful) thoughts about yourself.

You have to *believe* that you are worthy of feeling good about yourself.

It is a brave act: to stop running, to let yourself feel;
to watch all that hurt, and pain pour out of you like an ocean
and know that the same wave will never reach you again.

April Green

The art of surrendering

'Surrendering to the truth:

as it is

as it may not be as I wanted

as it's something I can no longer fight with

as it will free me to align with everything
coming my way.'

When you surrender control of life's outcomes,
things always work out better than you could ever imagine.
And even though you may not receive what you
originally wanted, you will receive something more,
something unexpected, something in line with
where you are destined to be.

(The Universe knows what is best for you.)

April Green

Surrendering control

'I can bring you the people and situations that are best for you' says the Universe.

'But first, you must let me connect to your energy. You must let go of trying to do it your way, the way you have planned, the way you want it to be; because this is the energy of resistance and it is blocking me from doing my work. You must surrender all control before I can step in and take over.

Turn your attention towards me.'

April Green

Untying the energy you have attached to people,
and things, and memories,
is one of the most liberating acts of self-care
you can ever do for yourself.

April Green

The art of letting go

When you focus on the person you want to become, you will very naturally, and very organically let go of the thoughts and beliefs that are holding you back. But you have to throw yourself into the person you want to become. You have to fall into them, love every piece of them, love every step they are taking, love every flower blooming beside them. You have to cherish all of the things you've never noticed before because you've been too pre-occupied holding onto the one thing that has already gone. It's the only way to let go completely. And remember— it is fear that grasps and clings; but it is love that lets go. When you understand this, the pain of the past will start to lose its power over you. It will shift, change shape, become a different shade, as you gradually experience the art of focusing on where you are going, and not on where you have already been.

April Green

You can't focus on two things at once.

All it takes is a simple choice, a simple decision,
to turn towards the better vision instead of
facing the painful one.

April Green

A loving reminder

The things you've hidden from yourself; the pain you've tucked away, the times you've swallowed your voice for fear of being misunderstood, the aching to belong, to feel loved, to connect with other people, with life. All the risks you have taken; the rejection you have experienced, the heartache you have gone through, are as real and as valid as the ground upon which you walk. And even though none of these things define you; none of these things are who you *truly* are, they have helped you become who you are right now. So you must never deny them or disown them. You must never keep them covered up. For they are your teachers, your lessons; they have brought you to where you are. And when you start to own them fully, honour them relentlessly, you will realise that you needed them all along.

April Green

There is a place in your life
that connects you to the person you were
before all the chaos, all the pain, all the heartache;
before you looked in the mirror and judged
the reflection looking back at you.

(You must find this place again.)

April Green

The journey back

And this is what happens when you can't take any more pain. When you surrender. When you break open:

You go back. But only for a little while. You go back: to the time when you were building your own identity; when you were drawn to what your soul was aligned to, when you listened to your own taste in music, wrote your truth in words, found happiness in the little things. You go back to when you didn't think too much about where you were going, but you lived as though you had forever ahead of you; where you ran, and stumbled, and fell through every changing season. You go back to before the world got hold of you; before the system, and the conditioning reached into you, before you followed the same path as everyone else. You go back. And you forget about the others for a little while. You lose yourself, but you don't get lost. You take the right turn: the one where the path is rough and crooked, and the flowers are wild and free. The one where you can be who you want to be, say what you want to say, do what you want to do, and love what you want to love.

You go back to the path that was always meant for you.

April Green

When you're on the right path,
you no longer need to navigate
through life.

You *become* life itself.

April Green

reconnecting

I am creating
the space
to live intentionally
breathe deeply
love without fear
and heal the parts I have
forced into the shadows.

—the inner work of freedom

April Green

Setting an intention to create
the space to reconnect with yourself
gives your life a new order:

your inner being starts to come first.

April Green

Understanding that who I am
is not the collection of thoughts
I have about myself.

Understanding that who I am
is someone I can define all over
again.

April Green

Relearning what love needs to look like
starts with yourself.

April Green

Navigating the world within

Starting a healthy relationship with yourself after years of unloving yourself is a slow, and sometimes terrifying process. There will be times when you feel too exposed, too overwhelmed, too exhausted, and you will want to run back to the world you'd grown accustomed to; back to the pain that gave you some kind of feeling, some kind of energy. But don't forget this world was a heavy world; and most of the struggle came from within. So you must now spend time exploring the world within.

You are ready for this.

This is the beautiful phase you once thought you didn't deserve.

Reconnecting with yourself, healing, transforming,
is a progressive letting go of all the limitations
you've been carrying around with you.

It is an ongoing practice of unlearning,
and learning, and re-learning.

April Green

Becoming a reflection of love

Sometimes, you will settle for the kind of love you think you deserve because it feels familiar: it's the same love you've settled for in the past.

But what if it's also because it's a reflection of the love you've been giving yourself? What if it's also because you are unconsciously showing people what you think you deserve?

Use this time of reconnection to start practicing self-love: start by forgiving yourself for ever believing that you are not good enough, even for yourself.

The energy of love is what we were born with and it doesn't ever leave us. We leave love: we turn away from it each time we go searching for it outside of ourselves. We see it in other people, and we want it for ourselves; completely unaware that in doing so, we're trading the energy of love in our hearts for the energy of ingratitude, jealousy, and disillusionment.

The kind of energy that keeps love locked inside our chests.

April Green

Beautifully free and fearless

The freedom we are searching for is the freedom to love and accept ourselves as we are.

When you start the process of loving and accepting yourself, you are in line with exactly what the Universe wants for you: to give you the opportunity to express who you are; to create your own life, to love yourself so fully that you are ready to share yourself, as you are, with others.

April Green

One of the greatest fears we all have
is the fear of not being good enough.

But you can heal that part of you by
understanding that all you ever need
is to be good enough for yourself.

April Green

Learning what love needs to look like

No one teaches you how to love yourself; no one shows you how to bloom when the sun has turned away and you're drenched in loneliness and despair.

Sometimes it happens when you become tired of the same stories, the same patterns, the same painful situations showing up again and again.

Sometimes it happens when you realise that you can't find any tender words for yourself because the negative self-talk is taking up too much space at the back of your throat.

Sometimes it happens when you understand that other people haven't been able to give you love, not because of you, but because they need healing too.

And sometimes it happens when your inner child starts crying out, because of wounds, because of injustice; and you're silenced into listening, silenced into changing, silenced into teaching yourself what love needs to look like.

April Green

Dedicate the space to practice being honest with yourself;
it will allow you to develop a much deeper relationship
with yourself, and the people who matter the most.

April Green

Honouring your wounds

When I started to understand the history of my wounds, I began to pay more attention to them; I tended them, nurtured them, lifted them out of the darkness. And in return, they honoured me with the kind of strength and wisdom I had felt before: as though it had always existed deep within my soul.

It is a fierce and courageous choice: expressing your fears, admitting they exist, listening to what they have to tell you. And the more you listen, the more you will see that most of them come from the wounds of the past; and eventually, they will show you that you have reached a place where you are no longer afraid.

April Green

Listen to the Earth
when she speaks
softly to you.

April Green

Listening to silence

And some answers will only reveal themselves once you have stopped exerting your energy trying to find them. Some answers will find you: in the conversations you have about the colour of sky when the sun falls upon the horizon. In the poem that holds you in the air like a bird paused in flight. In the silence between the Earth's sleeping breath and the dawn breaking open.

(Do not search for answers, search for the beauty in everyday life.)

April Green

Whatever your pain
feels like today:
I hope you are able
to turn towards the things
that nourish your soul.

April Green

Becoming as still as the Earth

And there may be times when you don't know how to say:

'I'm drowning inside, and my heart longs for something my hands can't reach.'

These are the times you must:

write
walk
breathe
curl up
read
listen to the ocean
feel close to the Earth.

For these times will pass; like the light of the falling moon.

April Green

To disconnect from your soul
is to disconnect from the breath of life.

(Stay together.)

April Green

Tender reminder

When things become too heavy:
you are allowed to remove them
from your being for a little while.

(Rest in the present moment.)

April Green

Days when my heart begs to be closer
to the heart of the things I love
are the days when I give myself
permission to become lost in my
own space.

April Green

Growing into a new life

When you start moving away from the overwhelming emotions of the past, each painful event takes on a different meaning and you begin to see the hidden lesson.

You were blooming all along.

And if the same pain,
the same problem,
the same chapter
returns
in a different light,
a different story,
then perhaps it is a lesson
you still need to learn.

April Green

Affirmation:

I allow
the present moment
to take me inward;
to the familiarity
of knowing who I am,
and not to the longing
for being anything more
than that.

April Green

If you keep projecting past experiences
and preconceived ideas onto the present moment
you will never get to experience anything new.

April Green

Remaining in the space of your soul

Turning away from the past is easy; for a little while. Staying away
is a harder cycle to break. You have to learn to remain in the space
of your soul: it's the only way through this new and wild path you
are carving out for yourself. And the further you walk, the more
expanded your whole being becomes. The wounded parts start to
heal naturally as they become free from the thorns of the past. The
things you thought you couldn't live without silently fall away.

The new life holds you in its gaze.

April Green

Your frequency shifts
when you stop allowing
old wounds to direct your life.

Decide which direction to move in.
Decide what is right for you; what
matters most to you.

Slow down.

Absorb the whole process.

April Green

Making your life a life

Unstitching the past from your bones is an overwhelming thing to do. It feels as though the thread of who you, the very thing you're clinging to, is being taken away from you; pulled apart at the seams. But it is not falling apart, it is coming back together: re-sewn into a tapestry of all the healing, and lessons, and strength you've built out of pain.

Letting go of the past is acknowledging that you deserve the chance to wear a new life.

Letting go gets easier
when you become consciously aware of all the things
you could have handled differently.

(Learn from them.)

April Green

Listening to your body

Some days, the light will start to dim, the moon will seem further away, and you will want to stay forever in that place between sleep and dreams. Other days, the flowers will curl around your ribs, your heart will feel warmer, and the sun will stay in the sky a little bit longer.

(Rest in the temporary phases—healing isn't linear.)

April Green

There is nothing wrong with falling back
to those in-between spaces
for as long as it takes to notice that,
even when the sky is at its darkest,
the light still shines
in places.

April Green

Healing from the inside

The internal transformation that no-one ever sees:

The promises you've made yourself stitched across your chest.

The lessons you've collected from the dirt upon your knees.

The courage to change rising like the sun in your bones.

The strength expanding in the spaces between your spine.

The wisdom drawing your eyes to new light.

The sweet, warm honey resting under your tongue.

The new life gathering beneath your feet.

The never-ending nurturing.

April Green

Note to self

Remember the words you whispered to your heart
when you were silently enduring each storm:

the kind words, the soft words, the hopeful words.

Remember those words and build yourself up from
there.

April Green

The scent of gratitude

The flowers blooming wildly inside you
are the ones calling for you to stand where you are
and look at everything you already have.

April Green

Gratitude gives you the space
to let go of the thoughts and feelings
that are causing a wall of resistance
to all the magical things coming your
way.

April Green

When you reach a place
where you can reflect
on how far you have come.

When you stop searching
for better, or more; and find
something to appreciate
with every breath you take:

then you are in a place of pure gratitude.

(Stay in this place.)

April Green

Sometimes, there are no words
to explain what your heart knows
to be right.

(Intuition is a feeling.)

April Green

Listening to the truth

If your heart's voice could be heard over the noise of the mind, it would say: 'listen to me.'

It took me a painfully long journey to understand that each time you go against what your inner voice knows to be right, you disconnect with yourself a little more. But your inner voice is your true identity calling out beneath the rubble of attachment, and limitations, and expectations. It is not the role you are playing, the stories you tell yourself, the mistakes you have made. Neither is it the inner critic who challenges you, contradicts you, causes doubt, and creates judgements. Your inner voice speaks the truth. It is the little whisper that walks through your bones every morning. It is the pull of awareness, the language of trust. It is telling you what is best for you. It is leading you to your purpose.

April Green

Alone is a place I visit often
to reclaim my strength.

April Green

reclaiming

You don't have to fight
to belong.

You are here.

Show up as you are.

(However that looks and feels to you.)

April Green

There is power
in your vulnerability
and how unafraid you are
of showing it to the world.

April Green

The power of honesty

The most important power you have is the ability to be honest with yourself.

We spend too much time protecting our feelings, avoiding being hurt, fearing rejection; we forget that speaking our worries out of ourselves is taking control.

It is allowing the value we place upon ourselves to be more important than fear.

April Green

All the things I was searching for were never found.

They were created from a power deep within me.

April Green

The inner work of freedom

A lot of the time, your life is not your own. It belongs to the lives you compare it to, the pressure you feel, the people you mix with, and the inner critic you believe to be the voice of reason. But if you want to be free to experience a spiritual life, then you have to reclaim your life as your own. You have to believe that you can create a healthy, balanced life from the inside out. And even though you may lose your way a little, feel uncertain, afraid; you are still allowed to stop for air, rest awhile, and soak in how far you have come.

I promise you will eventually live your way there.

April Green

We must learn to get past
the mental construct
of who we are expected to be
and spend more time reclaiming
who we truly are:

divine, individual, ever evolving beings.

April Green

Powerful reminder

In every given situation;

in every single moment life offers something up to you,

(positive or negative),

you hold the power to decide how you need to respond.

April Green

Affirmation:

I hold the power to turn away
from the things that are troubling me.

I hold the power to focus on the things
I can control.

I hold the power to build my own goals,
plant my own flowers, and follow my own
dreams.

April Green

Revealing your hidden worth

There is a moment—during the process of letting go—when you can feel your heart releasing its grip on the pain of wanting, the ache of longing, and the hunger for knowing. It is the moment that your true self; the self who is smothered beneath the weight of old and limiting beliefs, finally realises their value: 'I am worthy of so much more.'

April Green

Note to self:

My worth is not determined
by how other people view me.

My worth is determined
by how I view myself.

April Green

Staying in your power

People who don't have a high level of self-worth
will unintentionally project negative energy onto
everyone they meet.

Stay in your own energy field,
keep your vibrations high.

Remember that your opinion of yourself
should effortlessly overpower anyone else's
opinion of you.

April Green

Use your energy wisely:
use it in the direction of love, and gratitude and openness,
and this is what you will be surrounded by.

April Green

Stay grounded

The problem is that when we are faced with a difficult situation, we usually react based on how it makes the fragile, wounded parts of us feel, instead of allowing our inner being to deal with it the only way it knows how: to stay unmoved; to not be emotionally affected by anything.

This is the unconditional love you are searching for. This is within you. This is who you truly are.

April Green

The art of stilling your mind;
of not attaching any meaning to thoughts,
of turning your attention inward: to the ever-present stillness
that doesn't take you to harmful places.

April Green

In this life,
left alone,
things always work
themselves out.

It is the mind that gets in the way;
it is the mind that tries to control
the outcome for us.

And in doing so,
we never get to see
the outcome the Universe
would have given us.

(Learn to allow life to unfold as it is meant to.)

April Green

You don't suffer
with the thoughts your mind thinks;
you suffer when you get involved
with these thoughts.

April Green

Illusions shatter when you hold them too tight

We all tend to fall in love with the future too much: we fall in love with illusions. We grasp at them, cling to them, put our lives on hold for them, and always end up coming away empty handed.

The ego is a seducer—it carries us to a land of possibility: 'one day you will be happy, one day you will be loved, one day you will be valuable.' But all it is actually doing is telling us that one day, we will be what we have always been, but failed to see: unconditionally loved.

(Stay with the stillness of the soul. Don't get carried away with the ego.)

April Green

People and experiences
can only give you what you already feel yourself to be:

(worthy / loved / valued / happy.)

April Green

Accepting yourself as you are

Explaining yourself is a form of self-doubt and it leads people into thinking they are entitled to know everything about you.

But when you love and accept yourself as you are; when you have a strong sense of where you are going, and who you are becoming, the opinion of others becomes less important. No explanation is ever needed.

Where I am going
and who I am becoming
is for me to decide.

April Green

Learning to react in a positive way

Sometimes you just need to sit with a thing before you decide to act on it. Don't run, don't project an outcome; just allow it to sit alongside you as you turn your attention towards something else.

By the time you come back to it, the Universe will have already taken care of it, or it will have simply faded from view.

No one can teach you anything about healing
that you are not already going to discover for yourself.

But other people can let you see that they made it through
the same kind of pain, the same kind of heartbreak,
the same kind of trauma.

Other people can teach you how to be there
for the person walking behind you.

April Green

Use the way others treat you
as a reminder about how you need
to start treating yourself.

And if they treat you
exactly how you want to be treated,
then keep hold of that energy; turn it
into gold.

April Green

Some people will not support
your wellness and growth; but
that doesn't mean you have to
hold yourself back to make them
feel more comfortable.

April Green

Expressing your needs (first)

It is part of the human condition to have needs, and expressing those needs is being brave, and strong, and vulnerable all at once.

Never feel ashamed for telling others what is important to you; for defining what you need in order to make your journey a little easier.

The Earth will hear you. The people who matter will hear you. Your heart will thank you.

April Green

Keep exploring:

keep arranging and shaping
your inner belief system.

Remind yourself that you are here
to create a garden within yourself first.

April Green

Building a new relationship with yourself

Start cultivating a conscious relationship with yourself:

Be conscious of how you speak to yourself.

Be conscious of how the heart speaks to you.

Be conscious of what the ego is trying to pull you towards.

Be conscious of being here; of staying here.

Be conscious of being fully conscious.

April Green

Reminder:

If you are not centred within,
you will become totally focused on objects
outside of yourself with the expectation
that they will give you the balance you are
seeking.

April Green

Resetting healthy boundaries

Everything changes
when you rest in your own skin,
reset your boundaries,
focus on your vision.

If people react negatively
to your new mindset,
then it shows that you're
doing something right:

you're putting your own needs first.

April Green

Creating boundaries
to protect your emotional health
is an act of self-love.

April Green

Falling into rhythm

A boundary is not a wall;
it is a soft kind of energy
that you can mould
and stretch around your body,
and your feelings,
in order to articulate your needs.

Your boundaries should be in tune
with your purpose and journey in life;
they should play the melody
of everything that you stand for,

even when everything that you stand for
changes and evolves.

April Green

Seeking approval is not in line with your growth.

You have to drop the belief that you're not enough
unless you're doing something for other people.

When you live so hard for other people's
approval and acceptance,
you forget to live for yourself.

April Green

Nurturing who you are

You should never
seek approval
to be yourself.

It is not your job
to persuade people
to accept you as you are.

It is your job
to keep being you,
keep nurturing you,
and keep growing you.

April Green

If it doesn't feel right,
you don't have to stay.

(The next step is always where you are meant to be.)

April Green

Holding on gets heavy

If you are walking away
to preserve your energy
for what you deserve
then this is the right thing
to do.

April Green

Loving without attachment says:

'I see you for who you are,

not for who I want you to be,

not for how you make me feel.'

April Green

The art of independence

If you are waiting for other flowers to bloom, your petals will slowly wilt.

Each time you depend on other people to become what you need them to be, you leave yourself a little more. And in the process of waiting, and expecting them to change, your life gets put on hold: you miss all the beautiful changes already happening beneath your feet.

April Green

You can love someone
and still leave if you believe
the relationship to be less
than you deserve.

(Love doesn't mean you have to stay.)

April Green

Leaving some people and things behind

Broken things look different
when they're put back together:
the pieces no longer fit, things get forced,
nothing feels the same.

Don't betray your worth
by returning to something
that didn't work out.

Leave each passing season behind
so that you can bloom as a fuller,
lusher person than ever before.

(More love will come.)

April Green

You start to love fully, and fearlessly
when you are ready to share
all of yourself, as you are,
with others.

April Green

Letting go of beliefs

If you are holding onto the belief that you have to look, or behave, or live a certain way in order to be accepted by others, then you are creating a barrier to the life you deserve.

You are the only person who can prioritise and fulfil what you expect your life to look like. No one else on this Earth can do that for you.

(There is freedom to be found in doing what you love from the soul instead of from a place of obligation.)

April Green

When you try to live up to people's
expectations of you, you end up trying to live a life
that was never meant for you.

April Green

Owning your life

Too often, we hang on to the expectations other people place on us as though our life depends on them. And it's an exhaustive battle: trying to live up to who other people need us to be—it's an energy we shouldn't be tangled up inside.

Once you understand that the expectations people place on you only serve to highlight the insecurities they have within themselves, the journey of owning your life truly begins.

(But you have to drop the expectations you have placed on other people too.)

April Green

Be careful with the expectations
you place on someone else's path.

April Green

Happiness

One day, you will stop looking for other people and things to bring you the kind of happiness you are seeking. One day, you will discover that happiness is the way you express yourself, it's the honest conversations you have with yourself; how courageously you stand up for what matters. It's the struggle you've grown through, the steps you're taking; how faithfully you trust yourself to always find a way there. It's the ending of things, your commitment to growth; how freely you release the parts that are no longer serving you. It's the anticipation of a future you are creating. It's the unshakeable belief that you are whole, and valuable, and deserving of your journey. It's a living, breathing thing, an energy within.

One day, you will discover that happiness is never going to be a moment you reach, but a thousand different moments you choose it to be.

April Green

Don't get too lost in deciding how you feel
about a situation that is out of your control.

Focus instead on all the positive possibilities
that can come out of this situation.

April Green

Understanding your power

When you understand your power, you will understand that you always have a choice on what to focus on. You will make your own decisions, leave unhealthy relationships, and let go of everything holding you back. When you understand your power, you will become empowered—you will start taking responsibility for *every* aspect of your life.

I am wild
because I am
still growing.

April Green

reaching

Unfolding

Don't rush your growth:

no one saw the struggle
the most beautiful
flower went through
to reach its fullest bloom.

April Green

Believe in yourself:

look what you have already grown through.

April Green

Taking the first step

In order to grow, you have to step into the unknown.

You have to keep walking, and digging, and discovering
until it becomes known to you; until it belongs to you,
until you can hold every part of your evolving self and say:

'Look how far we have travelled.'

April Green

There is no time limit
to taking the first gentle step towards
your transformation.

April Green

Growing through the seasons

When you choose to give your life more meaning; when you decide to grow towards a purpose, you will discover new dimensions to yourself. You will see beauty where there was once pain, courage where there was once fear, and love where there was once heartache. You will look at how far you have come and see that all along, you were planting your own garden.

April Green

Be intentional with the life you are building:
everything you are thinking, saying, and doing
is creating your world.

April Green

Praying the right way

Whatever you are conscious of being, is what you will keep receiving.

When you are praying for blessings, don't forget to pray in gratitude for the blessings you already have. Because, when you are praying in gratitude, you are telling the Universe that you are conscious of having enough; so you will continue to receive more.

But when you are praying in lack, (please give me this) you are telling the Universe that you are conscious of lacking something, so you will continue to receive less.

April Green

All the women I have ever been
are lifting me up to kiss
the sun.

April Green

Living intentionally

Intention is the energy behind everything you do. When you live intentionally you are setting a purpose for your life, and everything you do will be in line with that purpose. If it is your intention to be open and loving, then everything you do will have an open and loving energy behind it.

If you decide to start living intentionally:

Think deliberately about what you want your life to look like, then begin living in a way that honours this vision.

Make conscious choices and decisions *for yourself* so that you are not led by the outside world.

Focus on what's really important to you.

Let go of any thoughts that are holding you back.

Keep building your perfect life.

(The Universe will take care of everything else.)

April Green

And when you love and accept all of yourself:
the ones who are destined to find you
will find you.

April Green

The people who allow you to show up
with all of your feelings, all of your stories,
all of your complexities, and insecurities.

The people who love your 'too much' some days
and your 'too little' other days.

The people who accept all of you,
all the time.

—the right people

Your truth will unfold
when you are true to yourself;
when you find what moves your
soul.

April Green

If you want to attract your soulmates,
you have to share your truth without
shame.

You have to:

write it
dance it
sing it.

Relentlessly.

Authentically.

Unapologetically.

And they will come.

As real, and as pure
as the rising sun.

They will come.

April Green

When you collide with someone,
trust the timing.

Allow the connection to be real,
and meaningful;
even if it lasts for a second.

(The Universe
puts people on your path
for a reason.)

April Green

Don't block what life
is about to show you
because you're too busy
searching for the answer
to something that has already
happened.

Sometimes things leave
to free you.

Sometimes you leave
to free yourself.

Trust the timing of everything.

April Green

You can't fight the flow of life.

Once you start opening up
to what's happening
within you, and around you,
you will start noticing
the divine timing
of everything.

April Green

Becoming her

When I started showing up
as the woman I wanted to be,
the world began responding to me;
showing me all the different ways
I needed to keep moving,
and healing,
and growing,
and stretching beyond myself,
beyond anything I had ever
reached before.
When I started showing up
as the woman I wanted to be,
the world led me to a place where
I could finally say:

'I am her.'

April Green

When I look at the steps
I have already taken, and
the steps paved out for me ahead,
I fully understand that I do not need
anything, or anyone beyond me
to validate my existence.

April Green

Finding your purpose

What you are here to do does not have to be for a living. What you are here to do is to find a way of living that aligns you with your true nature. Something that will keep you present, something that will give your life more meaning, something that will help you live in harmony with your soul. Finding your purpose allows you to focus on simply 'being,' (in the moment, in a state of awareness, in the space of your soul), which takes the weight off your pain, and allows your true self to speak without the fear of not being heard. Finding your purpose is a very magical way of transforming pain and loss into something incredibly beautiful.

Your life becomes more meaningful
when you connect more deeply with the life
you are creating.

April Green

You were created to create

You have to awaken creativity;
you do not find it,
you awaken it
by doing something creative.

And then it finds you—expands,
evolves, manifests itself
in many different forms.

But one thing is certain:
when creativity infuses your heart
with its intoxicating energy,
it changes you forever.

April Green

It takes courage to step into your own shoes
and live your truest, most passionate life.

But this is your birthright;
this is what you are here
to do.

April Green

Honouring your individuality

Leave the door to your buried life open: it's where the centre piece of your soul lives; it's who you are.

The best parts of ourselves are the parts we fight against the most—the parts we believe we won't be accepted for unless we fold them away; hide them from the world. The too arty, too airy, too emotional, too loud, too quiet, too individual, too sensitive parts. But these are the magic parts. These are the parts we must be brave enough to reclaim and daring enough to wear.

These are the parts we must stand up for the most.

April Green

Courage is:

walking away from
who you were told to be
in favour of honouring your soul
and becoming the person
you were designed to be.

April Green

You are here

You are here. And you have travelled here on your own. It was you who pushed yourself when the mind tried to hold you back. It was you who navigated the wild terrain that brought you to your knees, ripped the breath from your mouth, and tore you open again and again. It was you who survived: came away changed, altered, expanded beyond the point of no return. So it is you who must remind yourself every day why you have to keep going—because you want to feel that you are truly living. You want to know that you are inhaling every type of season into your lungs, every single atom of hope, and love, and faith, and beauty; and still have space to experience more.

April Green

How much more beautiful
your journey becomes
when you untangle yourself
from old wounds and narratives,
and step into a completely
different perspective.

April Green

Evolving gracefully

The story the ego tells you about what is happening in your life will determine how you experience what is happening in your life. And it will always be from the angle of fear; from how things turned out in the past.

But old perspectives no longer fit with the new version of you.

When you surrender to outcomes, you will get to fully experience everything life is about to show you; and you will see it unfolding through the eyes of grace.

You will start blooming in places your never thought you could reach.

April Green

When you have a strong sense of purpose
you will not be easily moved.

April Green

Reminders for your journey

It's okay to move forward slowly.

Whenever you feel stuck, look at what's in your way: what obsessive thought is blocking your vision? Let it go.

Problems are always taken care of when you stop giving energy to them.

Trust the Universe / God / the Earth / your higher power.

Don't bring old energy into new connections.

You have the power to choose whether you think about something painful for days, or put it to one side and think about the action you can take towards your growth.

Dare to open your heart without any attachment to an outcome.

Every day, you are a little stronger than before; even when you are resting.

It's okay if you're not yet where you want to be. Remember: You don't always notice the sun rising in the sky until, one day, you feel its warmth touching your face and you realise how much you have grown.

April Green

I write to help you feel you're not alone;
to try and explain the things you can't,
to let you know I feel exactly the
same.

April Green

'I think my soul has always known
where it was going.'

love,
april green

instagram: @loveaprilgreen

www.bloomforyourself.co.uk

— Acknowledgements —

Sasha, Rachael, Tina

&
A very special thank-you to my readers.
Your love means more to me
than you will ever know.

CPSIA information can be obtained
at www.ICGtesting.com
Printed in the USA
FSHW010504231221
87146FS